ISBN-13: 978-1-950311-35-4
AllRightsReserved@2019ElenaPankey

Contents

Holiness of Laughter	4
Cats of St. Petersburg	6
Cats in March	8
Kitten	9
Special Ritual	11
Balcony Flights	14
Journey	17
Arriving	20
First Night Out	21
Get a Friend	25
Puppy	27
Friendship	30
New Trip	35
Dog School	37
Communication	38
Circumstances	40
Parting	43
Devotion	45
Author	46
Copy Rights Page	47
Get New Books	48

Cat Tosha Laughter

Fun stories for children and adults

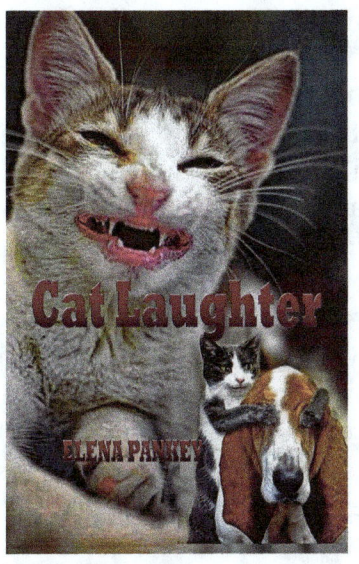

Elena Pankey

My relationships with my cats has saved me from a deadly, pervasive ignorance

Holiness of Laughter

Laughter is important for our physical health, and very useful to any person. Laughter reduces blood stress hormones, contributes to the production of good hormones and to the production of antibodies that help to protect from infection. Also, it helps the heart, vascular system, reduced pressure and increased muscle flexibility.

Researchers from the University of Maryland found that when people were watching funny films it improved the blood flow, strengthened the immune system, and made people more resistant to pain.

Laughter makes our life much more acceptable and enjoyable, at least for a while. It is an important tool for keeping our problems in proportion, to understand that things are not always as bad as we think. It is useful to try to find humor in any situation to bring you a better mood. Then, you could more easily cope with problems or fatigue. Humor and laughter can greatly reduce feelings of anxiety. It alleviates tension and increases our ability to concentrate. Laughter helps to stay positive by creating some pleasant emotions. When people laugh, they have a different attitude, better perspective, more hope for the best and just have a better rest. This is why in some special resorts laughter is used as a healing method for the rapid recovery of patients.

We need laughter not only for good physical health, but the ability to laugh is important for the soul. In case of a problem or awkward short pause at any gathering it is best to tell a short joke. And if arguments are heated, it might help if you would start laughing in a kind and cheerful sense, like you remember a good anecdote. Then you can find a more creative way to cope with the difficult situation.

Laughter brings people together, and this is its holiness. When you are in the company of others, it is good to tell something funny. This laughter will give you a minute of grace and cheer you up. Only when people laugh do they have pleasant time and remember it later. Sometimes laughter occurred spontaneously, unexpectedly and surprises us. But if you make an effort for your friends or family, trying to tell something funny, or read a good funny book, it's even better. We often do not expect laughter, just as we never expect grace or luck. The humor quality is very valuable. It is the greatest danger to take yourself, your own convictions and your own life too seriously. In such cases, people get sick. On the other hand, laughter helps us overcome many difficult situations. Everyone needs it in order not to take himself too seriously. Some wise man said that one should beware of those who do not know how to laugh and don't have sense of humor. The first sign of fanaticism is when people do not see anything funny in their surroundings. So often some troubles come from people who don't smile. They make you feel uncomfortable, and hard on the soul.

Humor is especially helpful in raising children. Children are very easy to manage when you put them in a pleasant environment with humor and laughter. Studies have shown that preschoolers laugh 400 times a day. Unfortunately, in adult age the frequency of laughter is sharply reduced. And some of us do not even remember the last time when they were laughing.

Laughter is a good instrument of love and loving people. It is the most important thing in a married life. If I can laugh with my partner over my mistakes, or on his mistakes, we will overcome any discontent or misunderstanding in any relationship. By laughing on something, we show each other that we are both imperfect and each of us has many sides for improvement.

This book is made for your enjoyable time and laughter.

***

Cats of St.Petersburg

For some people cats are like flowers. Some cats of the Sphinx breed remind us amazing tropical orchids. In this book, we have some funny drawings of St. Petersburg cats done by Tatyana Radionova, with some of our own editions. A wonderful artist Tatyana Rodionova lives in suburb of St.Petersburg, and with a great pleasure, she draws funny cats. In her house, those cats enjoy complete freedom. They go out and come back any time they want. In the winter, they bring their new friends to her home to eat something. Therefore, the artist has the opportunity to watch her "models" as she pleases.

Tatyana Rodionova devoted her creativity to cats. The artist's love for cats is an inexhaustible source of inspiration. This is why her paintings are very human, and permeated with love for our lesser brothers. When we look at her work, literally, our souls are happy and blooms. We see that the life of cats saturated with the same emotions as ours, human life. They also fall in love or could be sad. They also communicate with each other and educate their children. Her drawings look like a real cat theater. We could see different scenes from the cat's life, snatched up by the all-seeing gaze of the artist.

***

On the embankment of Admiralty in St. Petersburg (Russia), we could see several humanized cats, which are having fun. On the opposite side of the wide and deep Neva River, we could see the Vasilevskiy Island. There are also the Royal Palaces along the river, the former Stock Exchange building on the corner, and two rostral columns nearby.

St. Petersburg has many interesting architectural monuments, museums and cathedrals. During the White Nights of summer, all bridges over River Neva opened for several hours at night to let ships go to the Baltic Sea and back. On one of the embankments, we could see a granite monument of a Sphinx, which brought to the city from Egypt in 19 century.

Sphinx was a winged monster, who had

a female head and a lion's body. He stood at the gates of Thebes, and demanded a riddle to those who wanted to enter the city: "Who is walking on four legs, then on two, and then on three?" (It is a child, adult, and an old person with a cane).

The Sphinx killed those who could not solve it until Oedipus solved the riddle. Then, Sphinx vanished.

***

I have learned the wisdom of many philosophers and many cats. The wisdom of cats is immeasurably higher.

***

A cat and training are not so incompatible concepts. In just a couple of days a cat can train anyone.

***

It is very inconvenient habit of kittens (Alice had once made the remark) that, whatever you say to them they always purr. (Lewis Carroll)

***

The way to get on with a cat is to treat it as an equal – or even better, as the superior it knows itself to be. (Elizabeth Peters)

***

Beware of people who do not like cats

***

Those who'll play with cats must expect to be scratched. (Miguel de Cervantes) ***

Cats know how to obtain food without labor, shelter without confinement, and love without penalties. (Walter Lionel George)

Cats and Dogs

~
Adventures of Cat and Do. Black-White.
A Novel
Fun stories with funny pictures from the life of cats and dogs. Cat Tosha was thinking he was God, while making rules in a people's house. But once he visited Gelendzik, met local bully cats and fought for his life. After that adventure, Tosha came back to St. Petersburg to value his comfortable life. He began to care for a puppy Brake and made a good friendship with him. This book is about the specific characteristics of our most beloved pets.

About the Author

 Author has many years of job experience in different areas of art, education, literature, music, dance, theater, cinematography. She is a world traveler, wrote several fun books. While living in California, Elena teaching dancing.

Barcode Area
We will add the barcode for you.
Made with Cover Creator

Adventures of Cat and Do. Black-White.

Elena Pankey

Fun Stories for children and adults

Kitten

The services of cats for people are unquestionable, and their value is beyond doubt. Their main merit or the main cat profession is their hunting for rodents. But this useful activity has long been not considered the main reason why cats live next to us. Simply, we just love them, sometimes not for something, but, on the contrary, despite the whimsical nature, the undisciplined independence, and the not even too polite behavior.

Many years ago we lived in a beautiful suburb of Saint Petersburg. That was the northern capital of Russia and was considered the most western and intellectual city. Once upon a time, our neighbor's cat Murka delivered a lot of tiny kittens. Murka was full of deep love and care for her adorable children. Several times a day she carefully and lovingly licked them all over and was proud of her work.

For the first few days the eyes of the kittens were closed and they only sucked the sweet milk and slept all the time. This was normal, because on average, cats spend 2/3 of each day sleeping. This means that a nine-year-old cat is only active for three years of his life.

When feeding time would approach, tender Murka comfortably settled on her fluffy soft rug, and the kittens crawled and attached themselves alongside. Caring mother Murka blissfully smiled at them and quietly purred: "Oh, you are my little ones! Oh, you are my dear ones." A few weeks passed, they all grew quickly, and we were called to see them. At that time, my daughter Lila was already in the third grade. For a long time, she dreamed to have a kitten for a companion and promised to look well after him. Finally we decided to get a kitten, a lovely friend for her, and went to the neighbor to choose one.

The kittens were taken out in a large box and placed in the middle of the room. All these adorable kittens were colorful, fluffy, and extraordinarily amusing. It was clear that these big-eyed mischievous babies were very cute and curious creatures. Also, it was interesting that kittens always are born blue-eyed. But the color of kitten eyes changes at the age of three months, because the iris becomes saturated with pigment.

At the house of our neighbor we were joyfully watching the kittens, surprised that each of them had different color of fur. They slowly popped out  of the box and looked around with curiosity. Then, they quickly hid back and squeaked in a thin voice: "Oh! So many big people, and it is so thrilling. What will happen now?" One dark-gray kitten was the liveliest one. He looked like a small tiger with silky fur, which was covered with black and white stripes. A white speck was shining at the end of his nose and on his paws. The kitten quietly sat between his relatives, holding paws over the box, and gazed at us intently, muttering:"Well, consider something, at last! But better just take me with you, because I am the best anyway." We were surprised at his smart look, put him in our big bag, and carried him home for everyone's joy.

 When at home we opened the lid of the bag, our kitten leaned out with curiosity, looked around and approved the whole situation. Then, he loudly declared "meow," which in this case meant that he needed something to eat for the sake of his complete happiness.

At this time in the country was very popular children's song about a lazy boy named Antoshka. This boy did not want to do anything, saying that it was not taught at school. He did not want to help anyone, but he always wanted to eat. This popular and cheerful song had good teaching value. Everybody loved to sing it when it was playing on the radio: "Antoshka-Antoshka! Let's go to dig potatoes!" But Antoshka sarcastically justified that he cannot do it, because he is not trained for this work: "Tili-Tili! Trali-Vali! They did not teach us how to do it at school." It was funny and looked like it fitted our cat. So, we gave him that name Antoshka or, in the abbreviated form, just "Tosha".

Special Ritual

As we noted at once, our amazing Tosha was very clever and understood everything on the fly. In addition, he was the neatest kitten in the world. He loved to clean himself from all sorts of dirt of the day, spending many hours in this occupation. As a reasonable being, Tosha urged us to do it every day for our own welfare.

From day one we began to teach him how to use the toilet. I put a box of sand and some paper on the floor, and began to watch the kitten. After eating, he went directly to the restroom, like he knew that it was the correct place for his needs. Then, he began to fuss, trying to "dig out" a hole in the sand. At that moment, I picked him up and put on the edge of the toilet. He immediately did all his business there, jumped off the toilet onto a small bench that I set up for his short legs in advance. We helped him a little bit to do it, and Tosha quickly learned the lesson. As a result, since his childhood and for all his life, he has been accustomed to use a man-kind toilet. In time, Tosha even created a special ritual for it. Saying "meow" in advance, he opened the toilet door with his paw, jumped up, and did all his necessity, standing on the edge of the seat. Tosha was very angry and rushed around like a mad man if we did not wash it off immediately.

We loved and pampered our cat in every possible way, indulging his whims, letting him jump everywhere and do whatever he likes. Over time, Tosha became accustomed to our adoration and permissiveness. He was sure that he is a God. As a result, he took our attention for granted and was spoiled and overconfident. In all possible ways and at every opportunity,

Tosha indicated that we were only allowed to live next to him in the same apartment with the only one purpose: to feed him. Sometimes we needed to put him in his place, indicating "who is ruling the ball (or "who is who"). However, in response, Tosha became our domestic despot.

In general, he often announced to us about many disappointments in his life, especially in the impossibility of sole control of the world. Also, Tosha often stubbornly stressed that cats were the dominant and exclusive race on the Earth, and the rest of the world needed to follow his rules. But every ruler has a weakness. The main weakness and the biggest joy of our cat was his food. Tosha even preferred to drink

water from the faucet of the bathroom, and eat at the kitchen table, as any other person in the house. Also, he frequently by his loud meowing stressed the need to have his meals at certain times. He always insisted that discipline of his feeding on time was very vital to him. But sometimes Lila returned from her school a little bit later than usual, skipping the exact time of the cat's meal. In such cases, Tosha was very irritated and took revenge on the smallest member of our family.

It should be noted that all cats have strong organs of sense. They have an excellent vision, brilliant sense of smell and hearing, exceptional taste receptors. In addition, cats know how to distinguish between colors. All of that makes cats very sensitive animals. For example, cat's sense of smell is fourteen times stronger than humans'. This allows them to smell something that people don't even suspect.

Tosha always knew when we were walking from the elevator, by sniffing the front door. When Tosha heard my daughter Lila's approaching steps, he hid behind the curtain and waited for her impending arrival. Of course, Lila did not anticipate any dirty trick from a seemingly affectionate kitten. Therefore, his vigorous attacks were unexpected. When she entered the apartment, hoping for his joyful gratitude, hungry Tosha suddenly jumped out from the behind the curtain and rushed at her with lightning speed. Then

he clung firmly to the little girl's leg with all four paws, like to the trunk of a tree, scratching and biting her with all his strength.

Once we returned home in the evening and saw that my ten-year-old daughter was sitting high on the heater in the bathroom, shrunk as a small ball. She managed to escape from the angry cat. All this was bizarre, because, as a rule, "publicly" our cat seemed very gentle and affectionate. Furthermore, Tosha was fond of heights. Sometimes in the evening, he jumped from one cabinet to the other, trying to get somewhere high, and eventually he ended up sitting on the top of the door to the hall. His eyes shone at us with mysterious light. It seemed that he was ready to jump on somebody like he was hunting. We knew that the effect of glowing cat's eyes can be observed only in the presence of some source of light, even the weakest. But at such moments our little tiger looked threatening.

Tosha grew up very fast, more and more expressing aggression and inadequate social behavior. It was time to help him to become quieter. We knew that cats are more aggressive when they are not neutered, and it could be a huge problem. In the spring time such straight cats ("not castrated") become "March Cats"(as people call them).

We have already observed such cats on the streets of Gelendzik. In March they were screaming, fighting, and putting everyone upside down in their competitive rush or in a search for fiancés and brides. Every night they raised such a wild harmonic screaming that it seemed that someone was cutting them alive. This is why shortly after Tosha's appearance in our house we took him to a hospital.

Although the veterinary doctor performed the small surgery of sterilization very fast, he did not use an anesthesia. Tosha was screaming with the pain, but endured everything and survived. As a result of this operation, Tosha became phlegmatic, and an excessive lover of purity. He spent all his time at the window or on the balcony, watching birds or cleaning himself. He was no longer interested in dating the opposite sex, considering it all nonsense. However, all his life Tosha remembered his sufferings at the doctor's office, trying to revenge us for the painful stress he experienced in early childhood.

***

Balcony Flights

Tosha spent his childhood in St. Petersburg, on the fourth floor of our apartment. Since he never has been outside, he could not really appreciate the beauty of that sophisticated city. But a good weather he spent many hours on the balcony philosophically thinking about life.

Our small glassy balcony with sliding windows was like the universe, or a special place of Tasha's seclusion, education and entertainment. There, with a bird's eye view, Tosha watched what was going on in the world, got excited about the freedom of birds and tried to understand the meaning of life of some, less fortunate cats, living on the street down below.

Over time, his intuition began to tell him that there was something wrong in his body. That vague question was tormenting him, and there on the balcony he was looking for an answer to it. When we were at home, he sighed loudly and demonstratively, with all his appearance showing that it was entirely our fault. And when he did not see us, he still desperately and secretly dreamed of having a true friend or a good companion to talk to, at least, about his yearning for hunting.

Tosha possessed many talents, but hunting was his most successful hobby. When the passion for hunting or a desire for new knowledge, or a dream for travel overtook him, he would lean far out, looking around. At the same time, the main feature of Tosha's character was his longing to serve us and be useful to everybody. We even thought that before his cat's life he was a waiter. At least, our cat was deeply convinced that it was he who is the main breadwinner of the family, and should get at least some food for the household. Therefore, usually in the spring he opened the hunting season on our balcony (oh, sorry, on his own balcony).

Early in the morning, long before our awakening and rising, he was already bringing a sparrow to my bed. He did not eat it, but wanted to share his joy of his successful hunting. Also, it looked like he tried to please me, the one who was often strict to him and scolded the most. So, he was try-

ing to put the bloody sparrow next to my head as close as possible, so that I would immediately rejoice over it, while waking up. Several times, I explained him that I basically do not like fresh sparrows. But as all autocrats of "the higher race", he was very stubborn and confident of his rightness. He did not listen to my arguments, but continued to bring recently still living creatures, pointing out to us his personal usefulness in our family.

Also, it seemed that he had no height fear. Either he did not understand it or was not afraid. Sometimes he even tried to walk on the cornice, like in a circus, but without insurance, easily balancing on the narrow crossbeams. He was a risk-taking cat and longed for an adventure.

The sense of a balance in cats is well-developed. Their vestibular apparatus is located in their inner ear. When they are falling, they reflexively set their paws to the sides. This is how the surface of the cat's body increases, creating a "parachute effect". Then, they take in the air the position necessary for landing. Their very mobile tail performs a role of the stabilizer, while in tailless cats the whole-body acts as a stabilizer. Also, when falling from a high altitude, the cats do not land on their feet, but rather on their stomachs.

One day our fearless cat showed us all described above. He was so much involved in the bird watch, that he accidentally followed them and took off. It was a great test of excessive effort for him, but not because it was dangerous to fly from the fourth floor without a parachute. Rather because when gravity pulled him down and brought him back to the earth, Tosha suddenly found himself in an unfamiliar and even hostile environment. After landing, he was in a state of complete and deep shock, and quickly hid under the porch. We also were in shock, and tried as soon as possible to find him.

I really simply panicked after our "pilot" disappeared from the balcony, and began to scream to my husband to run down to find Tosha. Valery was

searching and calling our cat for a long time in the rapidly advancing darkness. But Tosha did not respond to his worried calls, probably because he was afraid to draw the attention of enemies. Also, he was sure that it was only our fault for his fall from such a cozy and safe balcony. He was trying to make us suffer longer and worry more, and punished us by his silence.

After a while, Valery found him near the basement hiding under the stairs, brought back home and washed him. After such flight and huge experience of fear, Tosha for a while stayed away from his favorite balcony. But the temptation to catch the bird was high and everything was repeated again.

For the sake of justice, it is necessary to say that every time, Tosha was very grateful to Valery for finding him and, most importantly, for washing him. After all that trouble, Tosha did not want to leave Valery's knees, and was cozily napping there all evening. Periodically Tosha even jumped up to my husband's shoulders and whispered something tender to his ear. This quiet purring sound filled our apartment with comfort and tranquility. Our smart cat was generously giving us the feeling of his need in us: reliability and warmth. Sometimes Tosha looked at all of us with his mystical eyes as if he would be saying: "Strive to the moon. Then you are most likely to be among the Stars." This was our slogan for a long time, and maybe because of that, all our dreams come true.

Spending many hours on the balcony, Tosha began to feel that he needed an active social life. After reflecting a little and fearing some new terrorist actions of our cat Tosha, we took him with us to a vacation on the Black Sea. Tosha was inspired by such a new way of life, perspective or adventure. He dreamed that the resort luxurious life will bring him much pleasure, joy and exciting events.

***

Cats choose us, we don't own them.
***
Dogs think they are human. Cats think they are gods.

***

Journey

When I was only twenty-five, sadly, my mother passed away, leaving me an inheritance, a house in the south of Russia. Every summer I quit any job I had in order to have two month vacation, and went to my homeland to enjoy the very healthy climate of Gelendzik. Since my mother's house was associated with many bitter memories, I never stayed there.

Every summer I was looking for renters who would pay for the whole year in advance. This is how my mother's house (and because of my efforts) served and supported me for a long time. It constantly brought me income and made my life much easier than most people had in Russia at that time. During our vacation on the wonderful, warm Black sea, we always stayed at my grandmother's small and poor house, where I spent my childhood. But she had also a beautiful, big garden with many fruit trees, and we enjoyed it very much.

My precious grandmother Anna was a very hospitable and caring woman. She was full of love and forgiveness to everybody and everything around her. She always was happy to see us and always was waiting for our visit. It was her only bright light in her humble and lonely life.

However, from the northern capital of Russia, St. Petersburg, it was very expensive to fly my family to the Southern resort town on the Black Sea. That is why we always went there by a train. But Soviet passenger trains were not very convenient to travel on. It was just an incredible event if there was a need to move there with your pets.

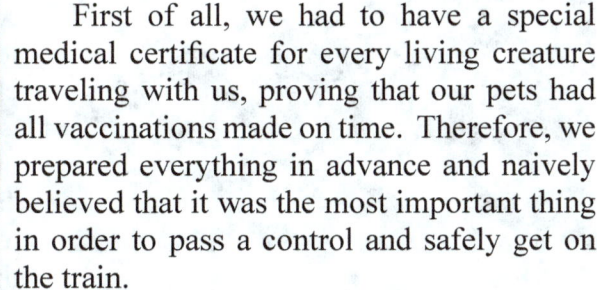

First of all, we had to have a special medical certificate for every living creature traveling with us, proving that our pets had all vaccinations made on time. Therefore, we prepared everything in advance and naively believed that it was the most important thing in order to pass a control and safely get on the train.

When we arrived at the station and found our train, we saw a huge crowd very slowly moving to the door of the car. The conductor of the train car was very shabby, and looked as if she wanted to bite everyone. But we wanted to make a good impression on her and made an attempt to smile from afar. By all our polite appearance we desired to show her that everything was in the correct order, and she would not have any problem to let us in. By our clean and friendly look we showed that in general it would be difficult to find any fault with us.

Finally, it was our turn to give our tickets to the conductor to check it out. Our smart Tosha was watching us and already knew that something was wrong with that conductor or with the whole situation. He felt that we were nervous, and as always wanted to help us. So, when we came closer to the train, he quickly hid in our large basket. We bought that basket specifically for this trip, because we planned to bring back some fruits, which always were difficult to find in St. Petersburg. But this trick with our brilliant Tosha's hiding obviously did not work. A train conductor, who clearly was suffering from a hangover, noticed a cat that had slipped into the basket. She suddenly hysterically screamed that the cat should have a muzzle in any public place. We never had such nonsense, and Tosha hissed and whispered from the basket: "It is she who should have a muzzle!"

The crowd near the train got agitated and looked around anxiously. Some frightened faces expected that somebody big and threatening really was there with no muzzle on and would attack and bite them. At that moment we realized that such exclamation and excessive noise about our little kitten was, of course, just a bureaucratic trick and a desire to get a

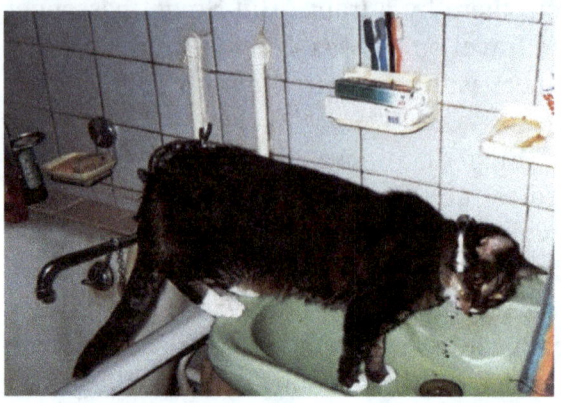

bribe. Realizing this, Valery quickly put some money in the conductor's pocket. Our witty Tosha added in a whisper that such conductor really needed it to get over her hangover and cleaning her brain.

However, that noise was upsetting and stressful for our "metropolitan thing", our intelligent cat. He did not like the unpleasant situation and conductor, who tried to dictate to us her rules. Most importantly, Tosha began to seriously worry about how he would travel for three days with such person in charge. He kept asking us by loud "meow", how in such difficult situation we will receive our legitimate daily tea, which was included in the ticket price. As already seen, this trip did not fore-show any pleasure or comfort.

Then we entered our train compartment and found ourselves in a very narrow space. We could not turn around without hitting each other. But at least we had a door for privacy, and immediately closed it. And then we released Tosha from the basket to the freedom of that small space. But Tosha did not express any happiness and did not jump around, as we had expected. Soon after, he felt strong claustrophobia, as we all did, too. In general, he had already missed his beautiful, clean home, where he ate at the table, like all decent people. Also, he missed his favorite balcony with exciting every day events.

This trip for our tender cat was also aggravated by two other reasons. First, as he saw, there was no one who planned to cook his favorite fish for him. As a result, Tosha was angry at the whole world, and refused to eat the canned food we brought. Moreover, next day he did not want to go to the dirty, public toilet in the vestibule. We tried to put some papers for him on the floor. But it only even more aroused outrage of our cat-esthete. In the protest against such inhuman conditions, Tosha went on a hunger strike.

Finally, we arrived to the city of Novorossiysk, which was forty kilometers from Gelendzik. We put the basket with the cat on the platform, and Tosha poured there a huge puddle of his three-day patience. It was his way of marking a new territory. Then, he felt a little bit better and all things went easier. We took a taxi, and in one hour of driving on the bumpy, curved mountain road, we finally reached the house of our dear grandmother Anna.

***

Dogs win your favor, but you try to get a favor of your cat.

***

Time spent with cats is never wasted.

***

Arriving

Our kind grandmother Anna was very surprised to see such a big group suddenly come to visit her from the northern capital. But she warmly and very cordially accepted us all, as always. Then, she settled us in a distant room with a terrace and a separate exit to the yard. That room, as well as the whole house, did not have any water inside nor did it have a toilet. All such common comfort was far in the garden, where we needed to walk a minute or two. But we were happy that our long journey had ended, and we could finally rest in a healthy climate, beautiful weather and swim in the warm sea.

We dropped our luggage on the floor and immediately started to cook the long-awaited fish for our hungry cat. While we were preparing Tosha's favorite food, of course, the whole district already smelled it. This delicious scent has notified all neighbors of our safe arrival to the resort. Tired Tosha was sitting next to the electric stove, licking his lips in the anticipation of a delightful dinner. As a being who loved to control everything, he carefully observed that everything would be done correctly and in his taste. Periodically, he looked at us, asking with disbelief if there really existed such an old electrical stove. To his surprise, he did not find anywhere a single balcony or a decent table where he would have his first meal at that new and pretty dusty place. Then he began to enjoy his long expected favorite and still hot fish. At that time, I cleaned the room and unpacked our things. Soon, after eating so deliciously, Tosha had a short nap in the southern warm sunshine. Then he recalled the main reason for his arrival and decided to look around.

Tosha was still very young and inexperienced. He knew only his comfortable life on the safe balcony of St. Petersburg apartment. But he, like any young man, was looking for something incredible, interesting and exciting. Shortly after filling his warm tummy with fish, the naive Tosha stepped resolutely into the unknown, into the dark neighboring bushes.

***

First Night Out

The owner or the boss of this area was the self-confident red haired cat with the name Vaska. This local "Mafioso" enjoyed undeniable authority among local cats. Around the nearby houses he had long established his solid order, in which no one dared to doubt, afraid of his claws and teeth.

One day hungry Vaska watched from the bushes for our unexpected arrival. He smelled nearby a new cat, a stranger, and was very surprised by such astonishing invasion on his territory of that "capital thing", a romantic Tosha. Then he enviously inhaled the aroma of the fish we were preparing (capelin, hake, cod fish), and terribly envied the wealth of the new holidaymaker.

At that time, cheerful and carefree Tosha went ahead, unsuspecting and not noticing that new, bewildering, unknown danger is waiting ahead. Tosha began digging a hole near the neighboring bushes, without suspecting any stunts of the local tycoons, and wanting just to empty his intestines. But suddenly, the impudent cat Vaska jumped at him unexpectedly and grabbed his fur and skin on the back.

For the sake of justice, or in fairness, I must say that the neighbor's cat Vaska was neither a strong athlete nor a muscular sportsman. He also enjoyed eating some good fish or "what God will give," he liked to sleep between the rare moments of hunting, sending his subordinates, younger cats, on his errands. Even though he did not have a special athleticism or dexterity, he had experience and smarts, as all other streets cats. In addition, the factor of surprise played a decisive role and he was helped by the surprise factor.

When Vaska attacked Tosha, our cat lost his balance and fell. But since he also was very clever cat, he recollected how he was jumping in St. Petersburg. Tosha in his mind saw a picture of how he was hunting from behind the curtains for Lila, releasing his claws at my defenseless, small daughter. So, Tosha recovered very fast and attacked in the same manner the local cat. But the local Mafioso, Vaska, even from the "lying" position, frantically continued to shove and push his legs, trying to hit Tosha harder. They fought for a while with varying success, because both of them were hampered by their fat bellies. Then, our intelligent Tosha recalled different methods of fighting he watched on TV, and it gave him more courage. Tosha applied the "furred paw of rage" and began to win.

Snooty Vaska could not bear that the stranger was fighting back. Feeling that he is losing the battle and concerning for his reputation, insidious Vaska looked around, but he did not notice the audience. Then he decided to escape with no loss from Tosha's defensive system. However, it was not in quarrelsome Vaska's nature to forgive the loss. He conceived the idea of defeating Tosha under other circumstances, more favorable for him.

In the circle of his friends, he began to conduct propaganda against "wealthy newcomer, who was spoiled by unknown and very delicious fish." Vaska tempted his rascal friends that when they defeat Tosha, they would

be able to take possession and fess all these "cod, tilapia, catfish and hake". Therefore, at night, he called his neighbors, gangs and all eternally hungry cats, who were not averse to "pound their bones". They came and hid in ambush around our house, waiting for Tosha. They called him "a metropolitan thing, looking for an adventure". On the other hand, Tosha was inspired by the first victory over Vaska. He longed for the new sensations of the night life of resort society on the Black Sea. So, on the next day he decided to continue his adventure.

As a social animal, a cat uses a wide range of sound signals, as well as pheromones and body movements for communication. Our cat Tosha also had excellent hearing. While watching our cat, we saw that he can sort the noise in any direction. Tosha could move each ear independently, turning it almost 180° in different sides, watching simultaneously two sources of sound. Generally speaking, scientists concluded that cats can recognize the strength of sound, its distance and height, and therefore very accurately determine the location of its source. Cat ears are so well developed that they are able, even with their eyes closed, to orient themselves in space and hear rustle or squeak and catch mice passing by. All these unique qualities Tosha decided to demonstrate to the local revelers.

A warm and pleasant evening came down in Gelendzik, and we took Tosha out into the yard. He rummaged a little bit of a hole there in the dirt, then looked at us and suddenly ran away to the neighbors. We regretted that we had not tied our cat to the leg of the bed and had not kept him at home, but it was too late. So that night Tosha again spent in brutal battles with the local bacchanals. And then, for two more nights our sleep was accompanied by cats' screams and the wild fighting for the sphere of influence, for a local beauty, or for a territory of control.

On the third night, we almost lost hope that our cat-sybarite will survive in these fierce combats and return home. We called him and called him, but he did not show up. In the end, firmly confident that the love of our cat for cooked fish will return him home, we began to cook it endlessly. So, the horrible smell of cooked fish was filling all surrounding. It gave us the hope, that this enchanting and overwhelming scent (from which all of us were already nauseous), would lead our even half-dead tiger home.

Finally, we saw that our very battered, but alive and not defeated, Tosha was barely moving along the street. He was dirty, lost half of his skin, but looked wise. Now he had learned about the imperfection of the world. And most importantly, he learned that it was not the world that he dreamed about on the long St. Petersburg nights. Now Tosha knew that the real world was full of cunning treachery, unfaithfulness, and unpleasant surprises. It was a world where there was a fierce struggle for power and the spheres of influence, and only the strong and insidious cats could win.

Our wise, but not broken romantic Tosha was spending the remaining days resting high on the roof of the house. He was hidden there from all external eyes by the apricot tree. Tosha had a comfortable position there, lying quietly in the sun and licking his battle wounds. He was now sure that it would be much safer and more pleasant to observe someone else's secular life from afar.

As a touring outsider, he was not accepted into the public life of the local revelers. Yes, he no longer aspired to this paradise, where nobody was even fed for free, as he had been all his life. The Black Sea resort brought a lot of disappointments and seemed meaningless.

During his turbulent epic in Gelendzik, Tosha reconsidered his own, so comfortable past life. He now believed in the value of what he had before, and began to cherish it even more.

***

A dog will not forget the owner; a cat will not forget his house.
***

Way down deep, we're all motivated by the same urges.
***

It is impossible to keep a straight face in the presence of one or more kittens.

Get a Friend

How people treat animals is an indicator of the soul. It tells about the quality of a person and his goodness. People should remember that their pets also have feelings and simple thoughts. Our faithful pets closely watch our every step, trying to please us with their love and devotion. Their inner goal and purpose of life is only to serve the master and make him happy.

At the end of August we returned to St. Petersburg, where it was already quite cold. Endless rain and wind knocked at our windows, and gray sky heavily hung closer to the ground. On the eve of winter, we did not open windows on the balcony anymore. Soon, trying to keep the apartment as warm as possible, we glue special paper to the frames of the windows and tightly close up and lock the balcony. Tosha no longer walked along the cornice, but just sat near the glass of the window and looked at the gray sky. He did not even see birds there. Many of them already had flown to the South. The time of his favorite hunt was over, and Tosha again felt lonely and bored. He looked more and more unhappy and became depressed.

In the evening, when we returned from work, he jumped on the shoulders of his beloved owner Valery, rubbing against his ear and whispered something sympathetic to him. It was clear that he complained that we did not give him enough attention. Sometimes, he was sitting next to the easel of my husband, and while Valery was drawing, Tosha continued to talk to him, recalling his childhood and counting what he considered our faults. He reminded that we refused to eat his fresh sparrows, and not always at the specific time served his favorite fish. And most importantly, he was subjected to severe trials in the journey to the south. It turned out that Tosha felt like an unrecognized genius, and whispered that we neglected to distinguish his talents.

As a result of his endless mewing and purring, we realized that Tosha clearly expressed the desire to take care of someone. Tosha did not find self-satisfaction in the surroundings, and missed his loving relatives, who spent most of the day at work. He wanted to have his own devoted and loving companion who would respect and appreciate him.

Tosha dreamed to have a true friend, with whom he would spend all day together, maybe even share the meal and sleep place. After discussing it all, we decided to buy a puppy. The German Shepherd breed looked the best among all choices.

Puppy

New and happiest page of Tosha's life came soon with the arrival straight from Germany of a cute puppy. Valery and Lila went to meet him at the train station, and Tosha and I were waiting for him in our warm, cozy apartment.

The puppy was amazing. He looked like a very intelligent, smart and all understanding dog. He had a very long and clean pedigree. His documents were in excellent condition and in his passport we found his English name - "Brake". So we were extremely pleased with the new member of the family, even though he had such a foreign name.

At first Tosha was also very happy and even inspired by a sudden change in the rhythm of his life. He was not even jealous that all our attention went mostly to the tiny and awkward puppy. The generous and already matured Tosha forgave all turmoil created by that soft, funny and fat boy, Brake. In addition, Brake also was very kind and very happy to see us all. The dog constantly wagged his tail from his excessive friendliness. But at the beginning, Tosha misunderstood that waving tail. Touched by the southern experience, Tosha perceived it in a cat like way, as a sign of aggression, which led him into tension and a readiness to repel the attack. But soon after, Tosha began to learn a completely different canine sign language and adapted to understand his new friend. He became accustomed to it with no hesitation.

Our cat had an obsession about cleanliness. Therefore, he expected that we would also teach the dog to go to the same "human" toilet, as Tosha did himself. But at the beginning, puppy Brake did all his "necessities" on

the floor. We just did not have time to run with him down to the street from our fourth floor, and the "necessity" caught the puppy where he was at the moment. Tosha soon noticed that the dog creates too much new work for him. Our excessive lover of purity, Tosha walked after the puppy and tried to immediately clean it out or bury it. But to his disappointments, nothing was disappearing anywhere.

After several days of unsuccessful struggle for the purity of the house, Tosha was exhausted and defeated. It looked like he could not even stand on his feet with fatigue and he had an allergy. Then Tosha simply stopped moving on the floor, it was already above his dignity. He began to just jump from one cupboard to the closet and back.

Finally, Tosha wanted to show puppy that he was a superior to him. He walked around the apartment with his tail lifted, jumped where he wanted, and considered puppy as his subordinate. Tosha insisted that we would establish some limits for the dog. Since we fed them at the same time, Tosha immediately refused to eat with Brake from the same plate. Soon, our cat felt even greater concern. The puppy was also very fond of eating, especially he admired cooked fish.

Tosha always looked forward to the hour of his feeding. He was well-oriented in tastes, distinguished between sour, bitter and salty. This intelligence was due to a good scent and developed taste receptors in his tongue. The procedure of eating was for Tosha a long and pleasant time. Our cat loved to eat slowly, with the understanding of this pleasure, thoroughly chewing food and enjoying every sip. He was always looking for a good food at our kitchen and sometimes tried to get it without permission if we were not looking. His tummy was getting bigger and bigger. But Tosha periodically was whispering: "If you are fat and clumsy, still try to make some graceful poses. This golden rule is known even to all cats."

The cold Russian climate, uneventful and not very active life- style have made our pets very hungry. They tried to beg for food when we eat, or get it everywhere they could, even sometimes illegally. Once, when we were not at home, our dog Brake (of course at the instigation of Tosha) opened our small refrigerator. He ate a whole month's supply of butter and cheese, which I had brought back from the Baltic States. Then he hid under his table in fear and did not want to come out for a long time. When we returned home, he did not run out to greet us, and feeling deeply guilty, he did not respond to our calls as usual. He tried to be invisible.

We lightly, but strictly, scolded him so that both the cat and the dog would remember that we all must follow the rules. The dog understood everything, but he said that he was seduced by the incredible smell, could not resist the temptation, because the refrigerator smelled so enticing and tasty. We loved our silly puppy and even though after that event we were hungry for a long time, we quickly forgave Brake's invasion into our food supply.

Usually, we fed our two friends at the same time. Brake quickly swallowed everything that was in his bowl, and carefully licked the bottom.

After this, our smart puppy lay down next to the cat's bowl, looked at him sideways, assuming that the food was more important to his growing body than to an adult and lazy cat. At the same time, Tosha ate with great joy, slightly turning his head to the left, then to the right, and did not listen to the wailing of the dog. Then Brake, seizing the moment, thrust his face into the cat's bowl. But the cat was on his guard. Tosha learned how to fight in the southern resort, and how to stand up for himself. In the response to such an impudent invasion, Tosha painfully clanged the dog on the nose. I immediately came to the scene, trying to save the puppy from the feline claws. But Tosha just explained that this was only a small warning to an expensive but ungrateful family member. Our naive Brake suspected nothing like this. He was simply stunned by such a rebuff and never again touched the cat's bowl.

Friendship

Once we were singing a wonderful song about good friendship, which would not be broken or decline from the rains or blizzards, and a friend will not give up. The real friend will not ask something excessive or superfluous. A good friend can always help out, even if something happens suddenly. At noon or at midnight a friend will come to the rescue. True loyal friends could quarrel, then make peace, and always be like "two peas in a pod". It is necessary to be needed by someone in a difficult moment.

***

In our house a good friendship between our cat Tosha and dog Brake was established from the beginning. It was our duty to help one-year-old Tosha to accept and love three-month-old puppy Brake. We also tried not to single out either of them with special attention. Where there is no equality, there can be no friendship. Also, good games unite people as well as they unite animals, so we tried to play together a little. Then our pets began to greet each other with their noses. Soon, amazingly they more and more often slept in an embrace.

Although the size of our dog was increasing every day, Brake still was quite a small puppy. When he arrived to us, he naturally took our cat as a supreme leader. After Tosha shared with Brake his adventures at the southern resort, puppy began to treat Tosha especially with a deep respect, thinking, that he might be a real hero.

On the other hand, Brake had one very important advantage. He was allowed to go for a walk twice a day, and even though he was on the leash, it was outside of the apartment and he walked with his beloved owner. That fact made Tosha feel that Brake was somehow a very special creature, because he never could get it for himself. So he began to respect Brake or feel that they might be equal.

Finally, the cold winter came to our city with its frosts and snowstorm. Valery was not officially working anywhere yet, but stayed at home and painted his drawings on the subjects I would pick for him. Therefore, his duty was take Brake every day for a walk. Brake especially loved walks in the early mornings, and felt confident alongside with his adored master.

Sometime, when Valery was out in the down town, trying to sell his paintings, it was my turn to take our dog for a walk. But if Brake suddenly saw his master, his joy did not have a limit. I could not keep our strong animal on the leash. He did not listen to my commands. Love and joy towards Valery was overwhelming. I fell down, but Brake did not stop and continued to pull me on the slippery surface. He dragged me a few meters on the icy sidewalk until he reached Valery. Then Brake happily jumped on the chest of his favorite person and thankfully licked his face.

Most of all Brake loved his walks to a special land, a big area of a wasteland, where his comrades gathered in the evening, also in muzzles and on leashes. But sometimes there they were finally released at liberty, happily running in the snowdrifts and mud, with loud barking chasing each other, or hunting some cute girl-dogs. Brake had no fear. There was nothing dangerous outside for him, but just joy of freedom and great space to enjoy.

When Brake returned home from a street walk he was accustomed to jump into our bath for washing. The bath tub immediately was covered with dirt from the top to the bottom. Then, Brake shook himself briskly, pouring the remaining drops on all of us. And then he raced to the kitchen to see what we would give him for dinner. After all these exciting events, Brake went to my room and heavily dropped himself down on his place under the table. And Valery had to clean our bath after his cherished dog.

Tosha watched it all with an expression of deep surprise and disgust on his face. But then, he was happy that Brake came back to him. Tosha joyfully ran to the dog, and carefully sniffed him from the head to the feet. He sought to find out what interesting things Brake brought with him in addition to some fleas. Tosha longed to know all the news that was outside. For him it was the world of fears and dangers that he had learned on the south. Later, before going to his clean bed, Tosha told his friend, Brake about his adventures on the Black Sea, and promised one day to introduce him to all he described.

Soon after that, Tosha got a new hobby and followed it for a long time. Trying to show Brake that cleanliness in the house is his top priority, Tosha tried to clean the huge dog's face with his little tongue. First of all, he tightly clung to the dog's neck so that he did not run away and then licked it, trying to make the dog perfectly clean. But he did not have enough saliva, and quickly got tired. In addition, he also had to wash himself.

All these new worries and problems really upset Tosha. Therefore, not able to cope with the incredibly time-consuming task, Tosha slightly bit the snout of the dog, while periodically pounding him by his paw. He clearly indicated that it would be better for the dog to wash himself.

And Brake being not only extremely kind, but also a patient dog, thought it was some kind of special game or a tradition of his new home.

So, he endured everything the cat did to him with an air of inevitability. But all lessons about cleaning, that our cat gave to everybody, did not pass in vain. So, periodically, trying to be grateful, Brake carefully took the cat's small head into his huge mouth and gently licked it, playing with it.

Although our Tosha was a very tiny cat compared to the dog, he was older and wiser than the puppy. And in general, life under one roof for all habitants should be as pleasant and comfortable as possible. In any good relations most important is the ability to compromise and to accommodate each other. Our pets understood this rule well and never quarreled.

In the winter, the apartment was quite cold. Most often Tosha slept between our bed and a little warm central heating radiator. He was very territorial and did not allow anyone to approach this sacred place. Sometimes, at night, Tosha even moved down onto Valery's feet, and eventually very close to his head. Finally, there Tosha felt great, as in a paradise. He was snoring louder than even Valery, but it was his night lullaby. It was somehow amusing and created an additional warmth and comfort. Then, Valery began to snore even stronger than the cat. Only I could not sleep with such noise near my head and moved to the other room.

When Brake appeared in our home, Tosha decided that he should be

adjusted for something useful. After a dinner Tosha more and more often began to jump on the back of the dog and stayed there to get warm. Brake did not mind, and so they spent many nights together. But sometimes the cat wanted to emphasize again who was the master of the house. He would go to the room where Brake usually slept, and lay down on the special dog place under the table. When Brake approached his bedding, he saw that an insolent Tosha already sweetly slept there. But most likely Tosha simply pretended to be asleep and peeped at the dog, slightly opening one eye. Because of his kindness, Brake had no strength to disturb the cat. He modestly somehow squeezed alongside, barely fitting on a small rug.

Despite our efforts, the cat always felt his privileged position and enjoyed it. The good-natured dog easily conceded to him in everything and recognized his authority. Brake sometimes had a hard time, but he understood that for a happy life in a small apartment, everyone only needs peace.

So the cat and the dog were friends, despite their incredibly contradictory characters. Their peaceful life has refuted the proverb about the warring sides of the two beings. And the old saying "to live like a cat and a dog" did not glitter at all with truthfulness. But we learned that if the cat's tail was at rest, then he was calm. If the end of his tail was beating the floor, he was nervous. If his tail was waving, it meant the cat was confident, like all doors are open to him!

But it is always different with a dog's body language. In dogs all is on the contrary, and their tail plays a different role. This is the reason why dogs so often do not understand cats. But I'll tell you a secret: there is no stronger friendship than "cat - dog". If people were so friendly as some cats and dogs, everybody would be living in a much happier world!

New Trip

Next summer we decided to go to the Black Sea together. But suddenly right before the trip to Gelendzik Brake got sick. It was a very serious illness, a plague. Since he had all the vaccinations done on time, we did not expect this problem and were very worried. Trying to save our dear, loving dog and cure this serious illness, we did injections for him every four hours and by ourselves. My daughter Lila was boiling syringes in our kitchen, then I was holding the dog, and she was sticking medicine to him. This treatment was long, but we could not postpone the long-awaited trip to our vacation house in the South. We also could not return the tickets and went to the train station.

With a big love for his dog, kind Valery spent three days and two nights with Brake in the dirty, windy vestibule between the train cars, continuing to do the necessary injections to the still sick dog. Brake's adoration of his loving owner was endless, and he obediently endured everything that Valery did.

Finally, we arrived to my grandmother Anna, but this time we had not only a cat with us, but also our dog. Grandmother Anna again was very surprised, but as always, let us to stay in the same big summer room which has all comfort in the garden. But at least it had a terrace, where the cat and the dog could sleep.

In those 1980's years almost all food stores in Gelendzik were almost empty. But there was enough fish in the Black Sea for everyone. Therefore, this time we also cooked capelin and hake, but now for all members of our family. A couple of times our cat still ventured to run off to the night, looking for useless dates. But Brake followed his steps and quickly brought him back home. Then our strict dog slightly scolded the cat, reminding him of the danger of walking alone. Also, Brake was not yet strong enough to go out with the cat to fight any one whom Tosha would decide to challenge.

Finally, he told Brake about the local mafia and his walks alone stopped completely. Brake barked all night loudly throughout the whole district, and local mongrels echoed him with the bitterness. This time instead of the cats' night concerts, we could not fall asleep because of the skirmishes of the dogs. But our trip to the resort town ended with no additional troubles.

Dog School

When we returned to St. Petersburg, I decided that our dog should fulfill his mission, and start to serve or protect our apartment. Therefore, for this very special training, we sent Brake to a Kennel Club. He attended it for a year supervised by Lila or Valera.

At the end of the learning experience, dogs had a special exam. They were put in a row and conducted a lesson of an attention and concentration. A special smart cat was ordered for this particular exam, but could not make it. On that day, Lila and Valery took our cat Tosha in the basket to the Dog School and offered to use him for that. For the test all dogs should sit quietly, without expressing any reaction to their natural antagonist.

Tosha felt very courageous like a very important general on a special mission. He walked slowly in the front of all dogs, and only his straight up tail showed us that our cat was slightly nervous. Obviously, any cat would be nervous in the line of dangerous looking strangers. At the same time, some dogs slightly growled and grimaced, but our Brake only yawned from the boredom. He graduated from that high school with a diploma and honors.

Later, we participated in different dog competitions and he always got first prizes at all of them. Soon his whole doggy chest sparkled with the rewards. However, although our Brake was very talented, he was too kind for a protective service or a guard dog. He had a scaring appearance, but in fact, we could not teach him how to be aggressive. So our dream of a dog guarding our apartment was not meant to come true. But we put a lot of effort and soul in the process of raising our pets and loved them.

Finally our devoted dog Brake, as well as our smart cat Tosha became equal members of our family. Brake was also like a child to Valery. So, my main goal (to occupy everyone with different business) was crowned with success. It seemed that everyone was happy. It felt that our peaceful and enjoyable life would be forever.

Communication

One day in 1982 Valery prepared a canvas and asked me to sit for a while with the kitten Tosha on my lap. Later I took this painting with me to California, as a single memory about our cat Tosha and our life in St. Petersburg. Twelve years after that painting was done, already in 1994, in my apartment in Kupchino, I took a photo of my granddaughter Marina sitting in a big chair with our old cat Tosha nearby. On that day Tosha just visited us because he lived with my ex-husband in a different place. Tosha did not want to stay on the chair, and was nervously waving his tail, because he was not the center of our attention. It was our last meeting with Tosha, just before he left with his adored owner Valery to Ukraine.

Occasionally people say, that some couples live "like a cat and a dog", referring to the irreconcilable hostility between them. But on the other hand, you can recall a children's fairy tale about how a hunter lost his mitten in the winter. And then he found it in a haven of animals of different species that lived in peace and harmony, and never quarreled.

When you observe your pets, you could see that cats and dogs have different body language. Often this is the main reason for their misunderstanding or enmity. They are real "foreigners" for each other. An attentive owner quickly learns it and helps the pets develop some respect, tolerance, and consideration towards each other. For example, a dog's wagging tail means greeting, but in a cat it means irritation.

When a cat arches his back and grumbles, he is very pleased. But a dog's arching back with a growl means that he does not have a good mood, and clearly is out of sorts. When animals adjust to each other's body language and learn how to understand and talk with each other, then they get along well. After all, people can also learn foreign languages, including the language of their animals.

From the ancient time, people knew if we want to have pets of different breed at the same home, it is better to bring them together when they are less than one year old. This will give them the opportunity to live in friendship on the same territory from an early age. In addition, cats and dogs like all children will observe adults and adopt their characters. Seeing kindness and love between members of one family, smart pet will not conflict either.

***

Cats and dogs believe politicians are like cemetery caregivers — they are on top of everyone, but nobody listens. (Rita Mae Brown).

Circumstances
No matter what our differences are, we all look at the same moon

At the end of the 1980's came a colossal change in Russia, known as a "perestroika". Nobody expected that so huge and seemingly strong country as the Soviet Union was would be broken one day. Many people blamed the Government for fatal mistakes they made and for destroying the well working system. It looked like a very hard time had come for most average people. It was a new era of enterprising people, but some just lost themselves in the new conditions. Some others were strong and energetic individuals and enthusiastically welcomed the changes. The most talented adapted fast and moved into the future trying to achieve high grounds. They went forward without looking back, building a new life in the face of new markets, new morals and new values. But many others simply lost their jobs and did not know how to live or what to do. People accustomed to the established conditions of life could not adapt and perceived new social changes without bitterness.

I also was part of that country turmoil, twisted and running "like a squirrel in a wheel," trying to survive and keep the good living I had before it. But on the other hand, my life also got the unsteadiness of sand and the feeling that at any moment all good things would end, and beggarly and joyless days would come back.

One thing troubled me the most. It was the feelings of the impossibility of long inner peace and happiness. That fear was mixed with nightmares and some expectations that an unexpected betrayal was about to arrive. I lived through it from my very early childhood. Later, I tried to forget the most tragic moments of the earlier days, when I was living as an abandoned child. But subconsciously I was always afraid to lose love and a dear, close person.

For six years of our marriage with Valery we lived in absolute happiness, as it seemed. He was a good, simple and patient person, handsome man with big beautiful black eyes. But even though he was a talented artist, at that time he was not able to bring us any income.

On the other hand, I worked too much. I worked hard and constantly in several places to provide the comfortable environment and the favorable conditions for the creativity of my husband-artist. Gradually my fatigue accumulated, and I more and more felt the burden of keeping our family together. Once my patience finally completely burst, and I again began to convince Valery that he needed to work. Then I demanded that he get some kind of formal job and bring some money to the table. He found work for two nights a week as a guard at a garage, but it was a very hard on him and soon he quit it.

Before "perestroika", I had worked in a school for some time. Also, I had good relationships with the director of the school, which my daughter attended. That school needed a teacher for a drawing class. Traditionally mostly women were working as teachers in Russian schools. However, in order to work there you have to have a University education. But still, the payment is very small for the long hours of that stressful job.

Valery did not have a high education or a special diploma, which would allow him to get that job. But I arranged that through my personal contacts, and they accepted him as a teacher.

The school was in the courtyard across from our house. It was very close and comfortable. Valery did not need to wait in the early mornings on the cold streets of a harsh winter to use the public transportation. It was not necessary to get to work by driving anywhere for hours, and he saved the time and money because of it. Also, I thought he would help my daughter at the school, where she had a hard time with the schoolmates. It looked like it was very convenient for all of us, if he worked cross the house.

But after half a year, I noticed that Valery came home later and later. Then embarrassed Lila finally told me that he remained in a locked classroom with her young English teacher. Soon we learned that Valery started a hot romance with this woman. It was a painful time for all of us, the time of torment and sorrow. I was deeply worried that we all were losing the thing of extraordinarily value for each of us: our family, which I had been building for a long time and with such patience. That time was especially difficult for my little daughter, who loved Valery as a father. For six years of her childhood she was used to a calm and kind person with whom she had very friendly and warm relations.

But one day our happy world collapsed suddenly without warning. I could not forgive his treacherous betrayal, began a divorce and asked him to leave.

At that time, I continued to work a lot, and often was on the trips with groups of tourists. To my sorrowful regret I could not keep animals at home. Our cat Tosha and dog Brake left us and went with Valery in his rented apartment. Later, Valery moved to his mother land - Ukraine. And for me - my job was my escape. I fell in it completely with my head, trying to escape all tragic circumstances. I was left with only one joy: to raise and support my little granddaughter Marina.

***

In ancient times cats were worshiped as gods; they have not forgotten this.

Parting

Soon after our divorce, my ex-husband's love affair ended. But our separation was painful for all of us for a long time. Valery often was out of town on his business while leaving our dog Brake in the apartment of his friend. Not having permanent housing and stable work, soon after "perestroika", Valery left St. Petersburg for good, moving to his homeland in Zaporozhye. After the departure of the beloved master, Brake was very lonely and very much yearned to see all his family members. But Valery did not contact me, did not leave the address of the place where our dog lived, and I could not find him. As I found out many years later, devoted and loving dog Brake could not bear the separation from his beloved family. He was sitting all the time near the window of the apartment of Valera's friends, did not want to eat, and was just waiting for us all to come back to him and be together again. He died shortly after from longing and a broken heart.

***

It was a time when Valery could not find any job at all and did not have any place to live. He left St. Petersburg soon after our split-up and went to his home town Zaporozhye (Ukraine) to live with his mother. Valery never got married again. He lost his muse, and never was able to create anything as meaningful and beautiful as was done during the time of his life in St. Petersburg. He took our cat Tosha with him. Tosha lived a happy eighteen-year life in the house of Valery's mother.

Almost twenty-five years after our separation, I found on the Internet my former husband, already a famous artist. Once Valery wrote: "The last three months was a very difficult time for Tosha. Even though he tried very hard, he almost couldn't walk. One day his back legs completely refused to move. Soon after, he climbed under the cupboard and did not want to eat or drink. It looked like he felt the approach of death and wanted to hide from it. I pulled Tosha gently out from under the cupboard and put him on the couch. Then, I lay down next to him and put my palm under his head. He was breathing heavily and looked at me with very sad eyes. I tried to console and comfort him for some time.

Suddenly, a few beads of huge, bitter tears rolled from his eyes directly into my palm. He did not want to leave me and quietly said: "Muur. Thank you for everything. I always loved you." It was 10:45 pm. My kind, old friend Tosha went away irrevocably...

I buried him near my house under an old cherry tree. Every morning, when I go to my work, I send him greetings. I tried to break off the thought of grief. I always remembered our happy times with our cat Tosha. But life was going on..."

Once Valery saw a dream, in which Tosha told him a story. "One day I was running a field, and flew into the grass to the very ears, breathing honey and mint. Then, I decided that in the new life (in the ninth), I would be the same cat, but only better. Some time ago I was a kitten, who did not believe in fairy tales. But here, in the Paradise for all cats, to the last outskirts, all doors are always open. It is always warm, clean and dry here. There is neither rain nor snow. We are all just common cats, and have common people here, as well. That Paradise is the grace for those who settled here.

But I wish to hide myself in the warm hands, that kind, soft and loving hands of my master. I remember him so well. So sorry I could not be born back to the Earth, to have his tender strokes. I wish to see the sun in the window, as golden as was the fish on my former platter. Once on the south I was running a field with flowers and fought the local cats. They are all here now, but we live peacefully. All is in the past.

Devotion

Dogs and cats could tell you many funny or sad stories, if you want to listen to them. They are full of feelings, endlessly trust and depend on people's kindness. Pets watch your every step and know you well. They are true to one who tamed them without any conditions. Their own world is consisting in serving man.

When you domesticate pets, you are forever responsible for them. In any sorrows your loyal friends always would be your joy and support.

In any circumstances, do not abandon, do not leave your pets behind to the mercy of the fates. Even running away from war, keep and protect your pets. They never betray you, but always will be waiting for you.

Get New Books

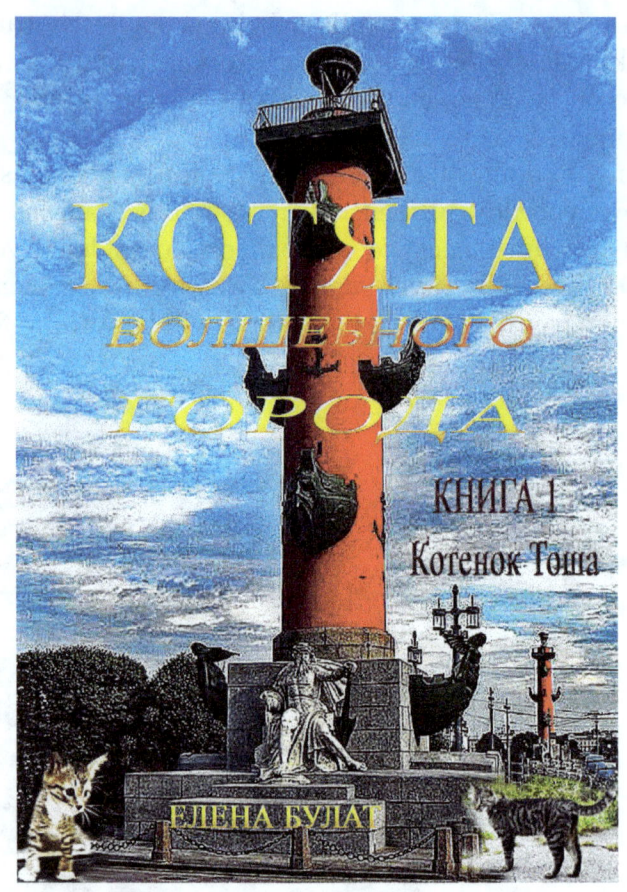

Monuments of Cats in Russia and the World
www.TangoCaminito.com

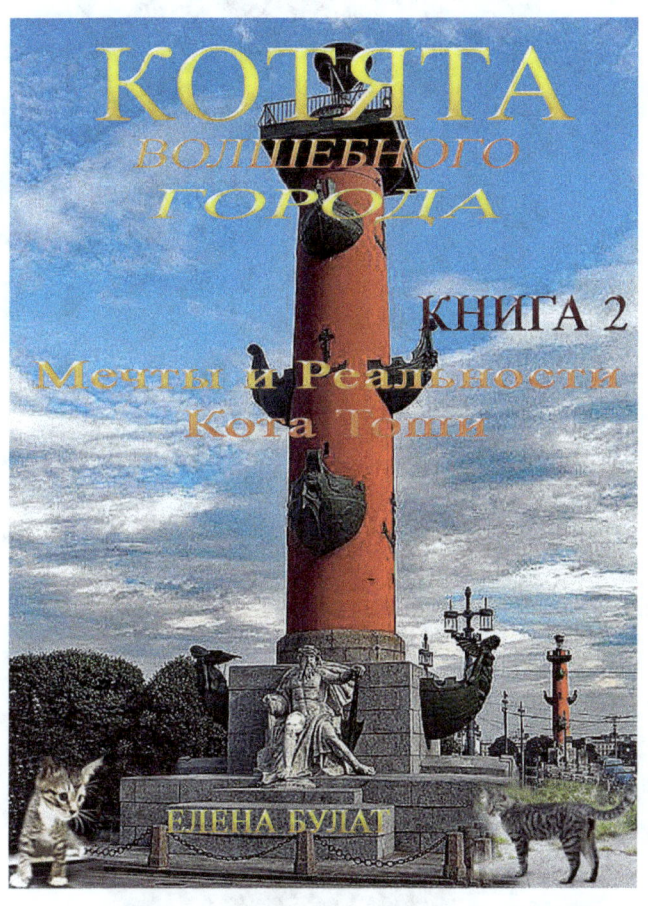

Book 1 and Book2 and Book3 . "Kittens of the Magic City. Kitty Tosha "is included in the trilogy about the kittens of the magical, Russian

Author

Elena Pankey graduated from the prestigious Leningrad State University as a philologist-linguist. She learned played accordion, studded different dance movements, including Mexican, African, Russian and authentic Gypsy dance. She had more than forty years of job experience in different areas of art, music, dance and theater.

She worked a sound assistant of the movie productions, radio journalist, and newspaper correspondent, owned her businesses and traveled the world. After Russian "perestroika" of 1990s, she moved to California, where Elena happily married to a wonderful American person.

While living in CA, she developed interesting hobbies, such as Ayurveda, Yoga, Thy-chi (studied in Thailand), Zumba, learned the healing energy of herbs and enjoyed gardening. Her main hobby was writing, traveling and supporting charity.

After 15 years of teaching Argentine Tango, Elena developed a series of tango courses that have helped people improve the quality of their lives and marriages.

Elena is an author of several historical books about resort town Gelendzik, where she grew up, fun books church art, Argentine tango and about her favorite pets. More: www.TangoCaminito.com

Copy Rights Page

Author is Elena Pankey. All rights reserved. No part of this publication may be reproduced, distributed, or transmitted in any form or by any means, including photocopying, recording, or other electronic or mechanical methods, without the prior written permission of the publisher, except in the case of brief quotations embodied in critical reviews and certain other noncommercial uses permitted by copyright law. For permission requests, write to the publisher, addressed "Attention: Permissions Coordinator," at the address: www.TangoCaminito.com.

The title of a book printed in the United States of America. First Edition was in 2019. Art work done by Valery Bulat and Tatyana Rodionova.

Logo, photos, images and design by Elena Pankey.

www.ingramcontent.com/pod-product-compliance
Lightning Source LLC
Chambersburg PA
CBHW052209110526
44591CB00012B/2145